universe
JOURNEY INTO DEEP SPACE

Dr. Mike Goldsmith

Illustrated by Dr. Mark A. Garlick

KINGFISHER
LONDON & NEW YORK

Copyright © Kingfisher 2012
Published in the United States by Kingfisher,
175 Fifth Ave., New York, NY 10010
Kingfisher is an imprint of Macmillan Children's Books, London.
All rights reserved.

Distributed in the U.S. and Canada by Macmillan, 175 Fifth Ave., New York, NY 10010

Library of Congress Cataloging-in-Publication data has been applied for.

ISBN: 978-0-7534-6876-0

Kingfisher books are available for special promotions and premiums. For details contact:
Special Markets Department, Macmillan, 175 Fifth Ave., New York, NY 10010.

For more information, please visit www.kingfisherbooks.com

Printed in China
1 3 5 7 9 8 6 4 2
1TR/0612/UTD/WKT/140MA

Illustration credits: the universe structure artworks on pages 44–45 are by
Julian Baker (JBIllustrations); all other illustrations are by Dr. Mark A. Garlick.

The Publisher would like to thank the following for permission to reproduce their material.
Every care has been taken to trace copyright holders. However, if there have been unintentional
omissions or failure to trace copyright holders, we apologize and will, if informed, endeavor
to make corrections in any future edition.

t = top; b = bottom; c = center; l = left; r = right

Page 11tr NASA/JPL; 12br NASA/JPL; 19tr NASA/JPL; 29br NASA/Goddard Space Center;
34br NASA/Goddard Space Center; 38bl NASA/JPL; 40bl NASA/Kepler; 42bl NASA/Hubble.

universe
JOURNEY INTO DEEP SPACE

KINGFISHER
NEW YORK

Beyond the Moon

On a moonless, cloudless night, far from city lights, the sky glows with the soft fire of a thousand stars. For millennia, people have gazed up into such skies and have been filled with the urge to understand the mysteries they hold.

This urge led to the development of astronomy, which in turn stimulated many other areas of science and philosophical thought about our place in the universe. But talking about space and looking at the objects in the night sky—first with the naked eye and then with increasingly powerful telescopes—was all people could do until last century.

Then, in the 1960s, human beings made their first small jumps into space. Within that decade, astronauts reached the Moon, safely returning to Earth, and uncrewed machines visited the planets of our solar system. Those voyages, and the continuing work of astronomers, have probed the secrets of our neighboring worlds and discovered many more beyond.

This book takes you to some of those places, brought to life by our growing understanding of the universe.

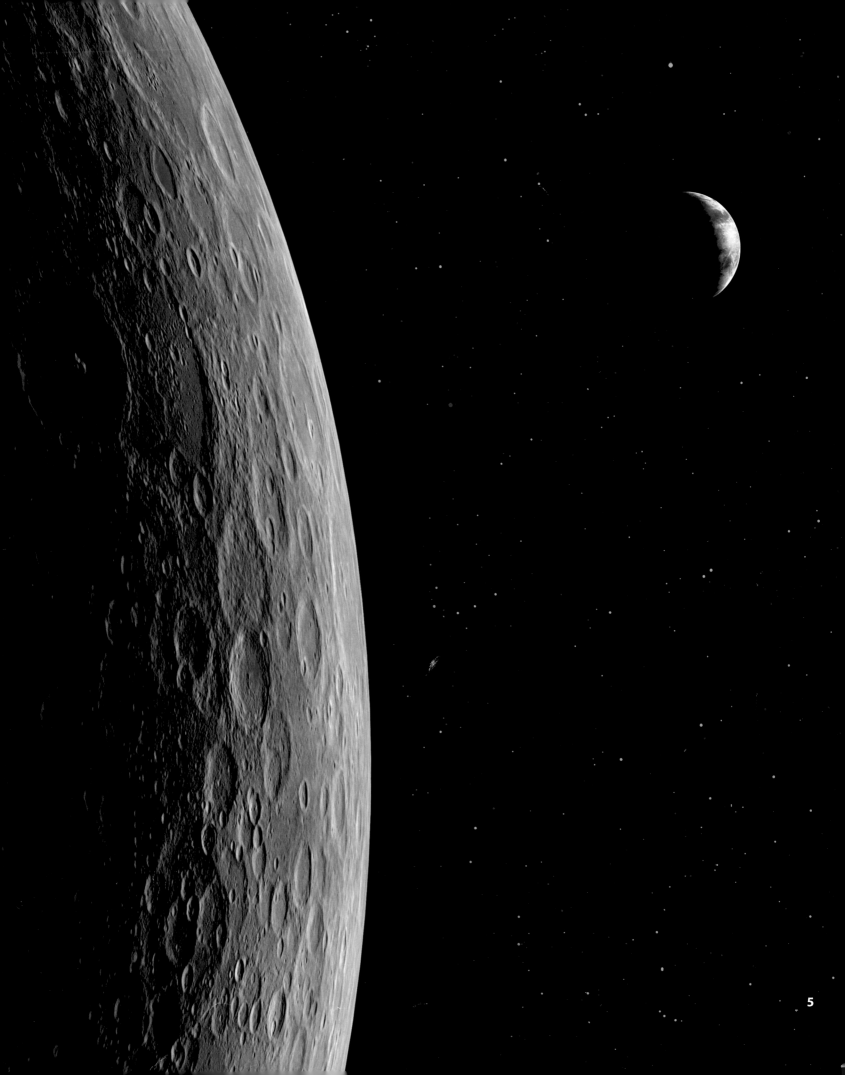

Journey into deep space

To make a journey through the stars and galaxies around us would, in reality, take billions of years—but in this book, you can leap great distances at the flick of a page. Because the distances are so enormous, we won't be measuring them in miles or kilometers—instead, we will be using light. Light is the fastest thing there is, and the time that light takes to cross the vastness of space is a useful way to talk about those distances. The Moon, our nearest neighbor in space, is 1.3 light-seconds away. So, if there were a giant explosion on the Moon, we would not see it on Earth until 1.3 seconds after it happened. Therefore, in viewing these incredible images of the universe, we are also looking back in time.

08: Cold dust
3–22 LMA

10: Hidden world
1–1.5 LHA

12: Gas storms
4.2 LHA

14: System's edge
16.5 LHA

16: Sister planet
20 LYA

18: Deep heat
44 LYA

20: Brown dwarf
172 LYA

KEY TO DISTANCES:
LMA = light-minutes away
LHA = light-hours away
LYA = light-years away

The speed of light is almost 186,300 mi. (300,000 kilometers) per second.

30: Ghostly hourglass
8,000 LYA

32: Star death
10,000 LYA

28: Lost worlds
2,000 LYA

34: Galactic heart
25,000–26,000 LYA

26: Twin-star sunset
1,670 LYA

36: Local galaxies
55,000 LYA

24: Melting world
1,550 LYA

22: Star nursery
1,340 LYA

Cold dust

3–22 light-minutes away

Leaving Earth, journeying outward from the Sun, the first planet we reach is Mars. Mars has been the destination of far more missions than any other world. Some scientists believe life existed on this planet long ago, when Mars was a warmer, wetter world with vast rivers flowing across its surface. Water may occasionally run there still, but for the most part, Mars is a chilly world of rust-red soil, empty deserts, and frozen water. Some of this water forms frosty patches on cold winter mornings such as this one. This surface rover, named *Spirit*, became inactive here in 2010 after six full years of transmitting information to Earth.

Hidden world

1–1.5 light-hours away

There are hundreds of moons in our solar system, but among them all, Titan is the only one with a thick atmosphere. Because of this atmosphere, Titan's surface can be seen properly only by landing on it—which is what the *Huygens* space probe managed to do in 2005. So far, Titan is the farthest world on which a machine from Earth has landed. It is a moon of the vast, ringed planet Saturn, which orbits about 1.3 light-hours from the Sun. Titan remains a strange and mysterious place, with murky "seas," black rain, and dark skies of ceaselessly rolling clouds.

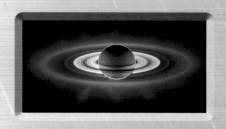

Huygens *was carried to Saturn by a spacecraft called* Cassini, *which took this picture of Saturn, lit from behind by the Sun. This view revealed two rings that we had not seen before.*

Gas storms

The solar system's distant outer planets and moons are dead worlds of gas, rock, and ice. But they are full of activity and motion all the same. On Triton, Neptune's giant moon, geysers of high-pressure gas burst up through the surface ice and surge high above the land. Once these jets reach a height of about 5 mi. (8km), they are blasted sideways by high-altitude winds. In the sky, the vast and blue-green globe of Neptune hangs, circled by ghostly rings. The surface of this gas giant is swept by endless gusts that blow faster than the winds on any other world we know about.

In 1989, the Voyager 2 *craft reached Neptune. Among its discoveries was the presence of both high, white clouds and deeper, dark ones in its atmosphere (above).*

System's edge

16.5 light-hours away

Out here at the cold edge of the solar system, strange, dark worlds of ice and rock drift slowly by on their centuries-long journeys around the distant Sun—a star that is no more than a bright spark in the black sky. So far, this is the farthest that probes from Earth have ever traveled, and it has taken them many decades to make their way here. They will probably continue their lonely voyages for thousands or even millions of years to come. There are four probes that haunt these desolate outer reaches, and two have fallen silent. The signals from the most distant, named *Voyager 1*, now take more than 16 hours to reach our home planet.

Sister planet

In our vast galaxy, there are billions and billions of stars, and around those stars orbit billions of planets. In all that countless number, there is a wide variety of worlds: giant spheres of mist, planets of ice and moons of fire, and asteroids of iron and gold. Among them there are lots of Earth-like planets—large enough to blanket themselves with an atmosphere, and with the right range of temperatures for water to wash upon their ocean shores. On many of these worlds a great complexity of chemicals exists and interacts—and on some of them, those chemicals may be the right kind for organic life to form.

Deep heat

Planets receive some of their heat from the stars they orbit. But most of them generate their own, too, from deep inside. There are worlds with barren, icy surfaces that conceal warmer liquid seas beneath. For life to form from nonliving chemicals, little more than warmth, water, and time is required. So, some of these dark and hidden seas may contain living organisms whose forms we can only guess at. Even on our own world, there are creatures who spend their whole lives in the volcanic warmth of deep ocean vents. They neither venture to the surface nor need the Sun's light to survive. If the raw materials for life are available, then life will find a way.

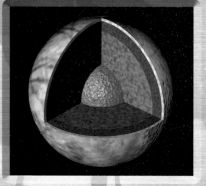

Jupiter's moon Europa may look like this inside: a metal core surrounded by a thick rock layer, in turn surrounded by a deep liquid ocean with a frozen crust.

Brown dwarf

172 light-years away

Not all stars are like our hot, yellow Sun. The Sun is a yellow dwarf—a midsize, middle-aged star that has enough mass to burn brightly. A brown dwarf is a faint and virtually dead star that does not have enough mass to support the nuclear reactions that produce starlight. Such small, low-mass stars could easily be mistaken for huge planets. The color of a star depends on its temperature. The hotter it is, the brighter its color. This brown dwarf (left) is a dim, dull, and deep-red object because it is very cool for a star—about half the temperature of the Sun. Its orbiting planets receive little light and have blood-red or crimson skies.

Star nursery

Throughout our galaxy, there are many dark clouds, often measuring dozens of light years across. They may drift through space for millions of years with little change—until they are disturbed by the passing of a star or the devastating explosion of a supernova. Then, parts of the clouds collapse, grow thick and hot, and become the birthplaces of stars—and of the planets that surround those stars. The dark clouds themselves are formed from the remains of dead or dying stars. This means that every new star is built from the dust and ashes of older ones. The same is true of the planets that orbit those stars and the creatures, such as ourselves, that inhabit those worlds. We are all built from pieces of stars.

Melting world

For most of its long life, this swollen star was similar
to our own Sun—a hot, yellow-white globe of glowing
gas supplying its nearby planets with light and warmth.
It has existed for ten billion years, but now its supplies of
nuclear fuel are dwindling fast. It is nearing the end of its
life. Enlarged to ten million times its original volume, it is
becoming a "red giant," and the 10,000-fold increase in its
output of light and heat is blasting and burning away the
surfaces of the worlds around it. In the very distant future,
our Sun and Earth will end in the same way.

Twin-star sunset

Most of the stars in our galaxy are not alone in space. Instead, they exist in pairs in what are known as "binary star systems." In these pairs, each star orbits the other in a celestial dance that may continue for billions of years. If the stars are far apart, the dance is slow, with each orbit lasting 10,000 years or more. Closer partners can spin around each other in a matter of days. Some double stars have planets moving around them. If you stood on the surface of one of these planets, you would see two suns in the sky, casting double shadows of different colors.

Lost worlds

After a star dies, the residue of its core is left behind.
Sometimes this remnant is so crushed by its own gravity
that it becomes a neutron star—an object made of
neutronium, a material so dense that 1 cu. in. (6.45cm^3)
of it would weigh 110 million tons (100 metric tonnes)
on Earth. Neutron stars have intense magnetic fields that
funnel radio waves into tight, narrow beams. As the star
spins, these beams shine out through space like those
of a lighthouse on our planet. If a beam happens to flash
across Earth, it can be detected as a regular throb
of energy. Such stars are called pulsars—and we know
that some have planets in orbit around them.

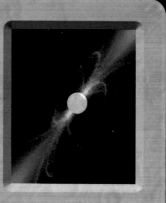

*The radiation beams of
pulsars are caused by
their intense magnetic
fields (shown in blue).
These fields are at their
strongest at the poles.*

Ghostly hourglass

Many stars survive for immense periods of time, bathing the worlds around them in a vast flow of heat and light energy that lasts for billions of years. But eventually the fuel that keeps them glowing begins to run out. In many cases, the star swells enormously, its outer layers spreading and thinning and finally forming a vast bubble called a planetary nebula. In this example, unknown forces have sculpted the nebula into the shape of an hourglass. The ancient core of the star, still glowing with leftover heat, can be seen as a bright dot at the center. Around it lie the shattered remains of ancient worlds.

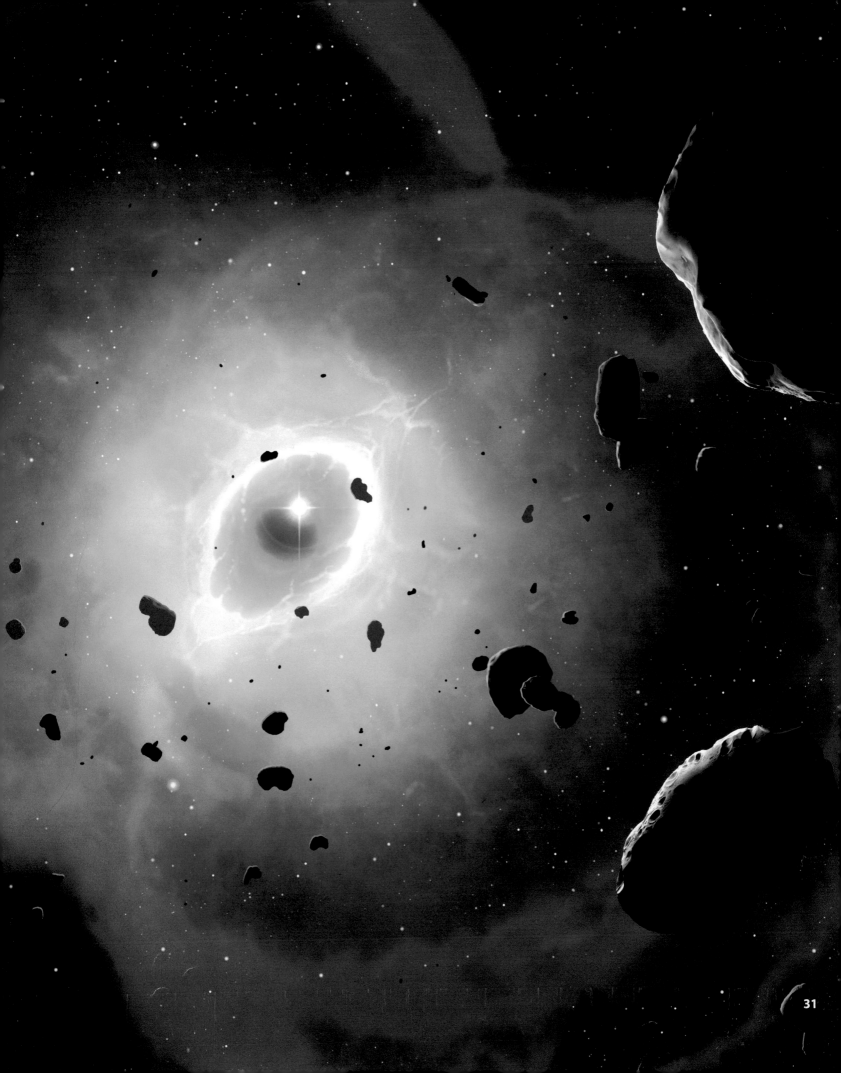

Star death

The more massive a star is, the shorter its life and the more catastrophic its death. For this star, ten times more massive than the Sun, its end is an extremely violent one. Its hydrogen fuel supplies have run out, and its ancient structure has shattered and fallen in on itself—drawn inward by the star's own powerful gravity and no longer opposed by the outward thrust of its fiery radiation. This "infall" is followed by an explosion so large that the dying star suddenly becomes a billion times brighter. The star is now a supernova, and all of its surrounding planets are either wiped away or flung into another region of space.

Galactic heart

25,000–26,000 light-years away

As the center of our galaxy is approached, the stars mass closer and closer together until darkness is no more. However, lurking at the center of the Milky Way is something very different from a star. It is an object of the same kind as that left behind after the supernova phase of the most massive stars: a black hole. But this is no ordinary black hole. It is a monster, more than four million times the mass of our Sun. The black hole is surrounded by a disk of speeding matter, all being drawn in by its irresistible gravity. And with each new object the black hole gathers and compresses, its mass grows even greater still.

Near the galactic center, the stars are very tightly packed—and mysterious. As well as ancient red stars, there are hot blue ones newly formed by some unknown event.

Local galaxies

Every star in Earth's night sky is a member of our galaxy, which we call the Milky Way. However, those few thousand stars that are visible to our eyes make up just a tiny fraction of the whole. For each star we can see, there are more than 50 million we cannot. The Milky Way is a vast system of stars, and it is just one of countless billions that are scattered like twists of light through the endlessness of space. Looking out from the galaxy's ragged edge, our nearest galactic neighbors—the brightest being Andromeda (shown to the right) and Triangulum (top right)—glow back at us across unimaginable distances, surrounded by the blackness of an eternal night.

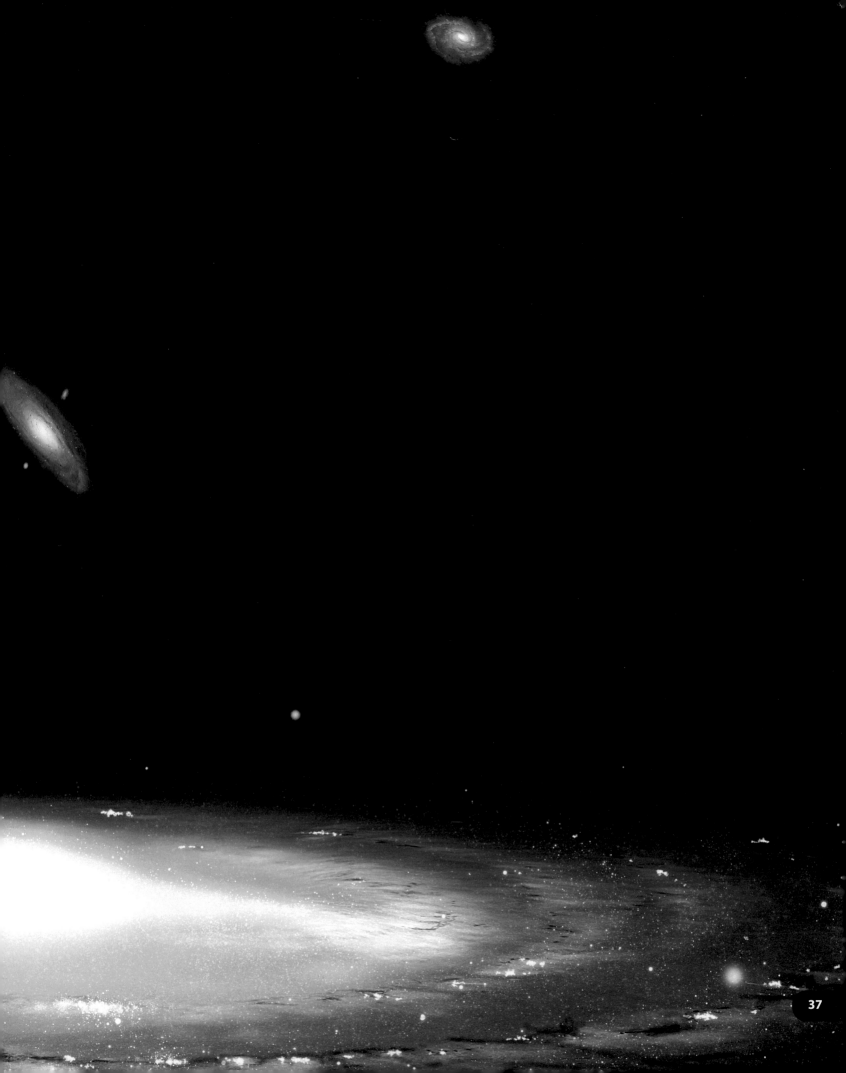

Neighbors in space

Words in **bold italics** are explained in the glossary (see pages 46–47).

EXPLORATION BY CREWED AND ROBOTIC SPACECRAFT

Throughout history, human beings have had a powerful urge to explore the world—to discover what lies beyond the next horizon. To satisfy that urge, they have crossed the lands and seas of Earth, and in the 20th century, they learned how to travel far beyond it.

Although no human has yet traveled farther than the Moon, uncrewed spacecraft have journeyed throughout the **solar system** to visit all of the **planets**—and numerous **moons** and smaller worlds as well. We have also learned that there are many other great **star** systems like our own, full of new worlds. One day, we may go to these systems, too.

*A Titan IIIE-Centaur rocket blasts off in 1977, carrying with it Voyager 1, perhaps the most successful **space probe** of all. The two Voyager spacecraft are among the most distant human-made objects ever to be launched into space.*

Cold dust

Mars: 4th planet from the Sun

Of all the planets, Mars has attracted most of our attention. With its Earth-like seasons and weather, its distinctive red glow, and its visible surface, it has always been a popular target for astronomers—and for exploration.

The dusty soil of Mars holds many mysteries. When it was tested by the first craft to land on Mars, its chemistry surprised everyone. Now, robots sift and scrutinize it in search of signs of life.

Like Earth, Mars has two **ice caps**. They are so cold in the winter that more than one fourth of the Martian **atmosphere** freezes solid there. In the spring, the ice turns back into gases that blast across the planet as violent winds.

Although the Martian atmosphere is far thinner than Earth's, it can support clouds and dust storms. Its color is caused by tiny particles of rust-red dust that float in the thin air.

Hidden world

Titan: Saturn's largest moon

Titan can seem very similar to Earth, with an atmosphere made mainly of **nitrogen**, plus lakes, rain, and even rainbows. However, it is unimaginably colder than Antarctica, with temperatures of around −330°F (−200°C).

Another key difference is that Titan's air contains no **oxygen**. Instead, it is laced with a fumelike mix of **hydrocarbons**, some similar to those emitted by car exhausts and others like those once found on the newborn Earth. The rain is a liquid form of **methane**, a gas used as a fuel on Earth, and the lakes are filled with methane, too. The rainbows range from deep red to **infrared** in color.

After its eight-year journey from Earth, the Huygens probe had enough power to study Titan's atmosphere and surface conditions for only a few hours.

Experiments on Earth have shown that the **chemicals** on Titan might be able to form living matter, especially if water deposited by comet impacts still exists there. The presence of life on Titan could explain why the makeup of the atmosphere changes so much close to its surface: **organisms** there could be converting the atmosphere for their own use, just as Earth's creatures do.

Gas storms

Triton's secrets lie in its origin. Unlike the other large moons in our solar system, it did not form close to its planet. Instead, it drifted in from the outer regions of the solar system to be captured by Neptune's **gravity**. On arrival, it may have destroyed many of Neptune's homegrown moons and used the debris to grow itself a new surface.

*The churning force of Neptune's gravity heated Triton on its arrival, melting the surface and forming oceans that may still linger beneath the icy **crust**.*

Triton's geology resembles that of Earth: it has valleys and mountains, volcano-like **geysers**, and few craters. But while on Earth it is **molten rock** that is geology's tool, on Titan it is water and liquefied **ammonia** gas that sculpt and animate the surface.

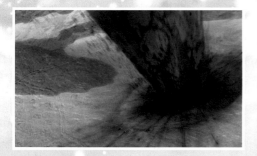

Triton's gas geysers are found in an area where the distant Sun often shines brightly. Although the heating effect is small, it is just enough to turn buried nitrogen ice into gas, which bursts up through the surface and fountains high into the black sky.

System's edge

Outer rim of the solar system

Most of the solar system's worlds are mysterious and distant. It is only Earth and the seven other planets that huddle "close" to the Sun, orbiting within about 2.8 billion mi. (4.5 billion km).

Beyond Neptune is a disk-shaped area called the **Kuiper belt**. Outside that belt is a vast, hollow, ball-shaped cloud known as the **Oort cloud**. Comets come from these distant regions, so it is thought that many of the worlds there are like them—great "spacebergs" of ice and grit. Most of them are much smaller than Earth—so small, in fact, that their weak gravity cannot draw them into planetlike spheres. But we know of a handful of larger **dwarf planets**, too. There may well be many more, lost in darkness and distance.

Beyond the Kuiper belt, the Sun looks very distant and remote. It provides hardly any heat in these dark regions.

*Everything in the outer solar system **orbits** the Sun, but the pull of its gravity is so weak—and the distances around the Sun are so great—that a year on this dwarf planet takes centuries to pass.*

Sister planet

A rocky, habitable world

Are we alone? It is one of the greatest questions we can ever ask. If the answer is "yes," then we will have to face the fact that we are unique in the entire, vast universe. If the answer is "no," then somewhere there are alien creatures existing on other worlds, and someday we might encounter them. So both answers carry a great significance for human beings.

Until the 1990s, we did not know of any planets beyond Neptune, but hundreds have now been discovered. It is thought that most stars have planets.

Living things on another world might look and behave very differently from Earth's organisms. We might not even recognize them as being alive.

What we do know is that if the right raw materials and conditions are present, then the building blocks of life will be produced by simple chemical reactions, and living **cells** will soon follow. What we do not know is how rare those materials and conditions are.

The nearest Earth-like world is so far away that we cannot hope to travel there for many thousands of years. Perhaps we never will. However, radio signals can cross entire **galaxies**. Using equipment on Earth, we can listen for messages coming from great distances. But, so far, all is silent.

Worlds beyond

Words in **bold italics** are explained in the glossary (see pages 46–47).

EXPLORATION BY OBSERVATION

We use telescopes to transform the faintest smudges of light in the night sky into vast galaxies. Not only do they capture millions of times more light than our eyes can, but they are also able to collect light from the same object for many hours—something our eyes can do for only a fraction of a second.

Human eyes have other limitations, too. In particular, they can see only light. Telescopes can detect a far wider range of *radiation*, from radio waves to gamma rays. Thanks to their enormous powers, telescopes are by far the most important source of information about the stars.

The best place to see the stars is outside the atmosphere, where there is no air to distort the view and cause stars to twinkle. This is the Kepler space observatory (below), which is in orbit around the Sun. It is searching for planets with Earth-like characteristics.

Deep heat

Life beneath an icy crust

A great many worlds are much hotter inside than out. For moons in close orbit around their planets, the main cause is gravitational—the shifting pull of gravity exerts churning forces deep inside them, and this results in heat.

Some of the larger moons in our solar system may have oceans beneath their icy surfaces: Callisto, Enceladus, Europa, and Ganymede are the most likely candidates. These oceans would be kept liquid by the gravitational heating described above. As well as preventing the water from freezing, this heat might possibly support life.

Alien life forms would need to take in energy to survive—perhaps from sunlight, food, or both.

When a liquid starts to freeze, its solid form usually sinks. But ice (frozen water) is different: it floats on liquid water, so under-ice seas can be stable.

Brown dwarf

A cool star with low mass

Brown dwarfs are objects that formed with a *mass* that is somewhere between that of a large planet and that of a small star. Because of this lower mass, the process of *nuclear fusion* either never got started in their *core* or quickly died away. This is why they are often referred to as "failed stars." They are very dim because they are unable to give out as much light and heat energy as regular stars. This makes them more difficult to find and study.

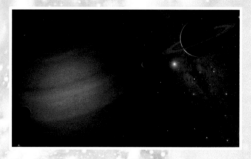

The planets in brown dwarf systems are closer to their stars than those in our solar system.

Brown dwarfs are so low in temperature that, in many ways, they are similar in nature to planets. They may have clouds and weather systems, similar to the "gas giant" planets in our solar system. They range in mass from around 15 to 75 times that of Jupiter. (Jupiter is the largest planet in our solar system. It is more than twice as massive as all of the other planets combined, and about 318 times more massive than Earth.) Strangely, despite this wide range of different masses, they are all roughly the same size as Jupiter, with a diameter of about 88,850 mi. (143,000km).

Star nursery

The Orion Nebula is truly massive—it is about 2,000 times the mass of the Sun. However, most of this mass is spread out very thinly: the **nebula** is about 25 light years across. It is by far the closest large star-forming region to the solar system.

The intricate patterns of dust and gas that form the nebula shelter at least 700 stars. These are in many different stages of development. Some of them are only a few thousand years old—perhaps a millionth of the way through their lives. In terms of a human lifespan, they are like one-hour-old babies.

*The colors of the nebula help tell us what it is made of. The redder areas (above) indicate the presence of hot **hydrogen** gas.*

Some of the stars in Orion's central regions are very massive, which means they burn very brightly. The intense radiation that surges out from them has the power to thrust gas and dust away from their neighborhoods. This process has swept clean the core (central region) of the nebula, leaving the stars there visible from Earth. These same stars will end their lives violently as **supernovas** ejecting most of their mass outward. These spectacular events help recycle stellar materials and may trigger the births of brand-new generations of stars.

Melting world

Most stars are powered by nuclear fusion—the special process in which hydrogen atoms combine to form **helium**. This process releases a great deal of energy, which we see as sunlight and starlight.

The core of a star is the hottest, densest part, so this is where fusion normally takes place. But the hydrogen there runs out eventually. Then the core begins to shrink, and temperatures and pressures increase, triggering fusion in a shell around the core.

Because the shell's volume is much larger than the core's, there are far more fusion reactions—so the star's emissions of energy increase enormously. This forces its atmosphere to expand very rapidly.

*As a star swells up to become a red giant, its atmosphere has less than one-millionth of the **density** it once had.*

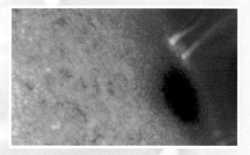

*Like the Sun, red giants have cooler dark spots, caused by **magnetic field** effects. These spots can be enormous, far larger than sunspots (the Sun's cooler areas).*

Twin-star sunset

A binary star system is one in which there are two stars. Each star orbits (travels around) the other. Binaries are very common. In fact, it may be that there are more stars in binaries than there are stars on their own.

Often, the stars in binary systems are very different from each other. Their color indicates temperature: one of them may be blue-white (hot), while the other could be orange (cool).

A number of binary stars are known to have planets in orbit around them. The planets may orbit either one or both of the stars. It is even possible for groups of three stars to have planets circling around them.

Planets of a binary system are likely to suffer extremes of temperature. At times, their surfaces may soften or melt in the heat. Any liquid may evaporate.

Although it is unlikely that a planet in a binary star system could be similar enough to Earth to support life, scientific calculations have shown that it is not impossible.

Across the galaxy

Words in **bold italics** are explained in the glossary (see pages 46–47).

EXPLORATION BY CALCULATION

As we look far out into space, there are more and more strange objects and events to be seen: exploding stars, black holes, cosmic lighthouses (or **pulsars**), and more. To explain them, advanced scientific theories are required. Fortunately, the scientific laws that apply within our solar system also hold true throughout the rest of the universe.

But still there are many things we do not understand, including a very basic question: what is the universe actually made of? We know that most of the universe is invisible, made up of "dark matter" and "dark energy" that we cannot see. Although we have some ideas about what dark matter may be, we know almost nothing about the nature of dark energy.

We have not yet defined exactly what dark matter is, but we know that it must exist. This cluster of stars—known as the Bullet Cluster—is held together by it.

Lost worlds

Planets orbiting a pulsar

In 1967, astronomers were baffled by a series of regular radio "beeps" arriving from an unknown region of space at a rate of one every 1.3 seconds. Some thought the beeps might be a message sent by the creatures of another world.

In fact, the signals are coming from a strange and ancient object: the core of a dead star. This core is tiny, very dense, and fast-spinning, with a powerful magnetic field that squirts out beams of radio waves. As the star spins, the beams wheel through space and sweep across Earth. Each beep, detected by astronomers, represents a single crossing of our planet. A small number of spinning neutron stars (or pulsars) send out beams of light or other types of radiation, as well as radio beams.

We know that some pulsars have planets orbiting them. Those planets must have had violent histories, since pulsars are formed in supernovae.

*Here, outflowing particles from the pulsar are interacting with a planet's magnetic field and atmosphere, causing spectacular **auroras** above the planet's magnetic poles.*

Ghostly hourglass

A planetary nebula

Planetary nebulae get their name from the fact that some of them are spherical (ball-shaped), and so they can look like planets when viewed from Earth. But, in fact, most are twisted into more complex shapes.

*The Hourglass, as it has been nicknamed, is a very new nebula. Its central **white dwarf** is only just beginning to form.*

The glowing gases inside the nebula can be seen here (above) in different colors. These colors are very useful because they tell us which **chemical elements** are present. Nitrogen shows up in red, hydrogen in green, and oxygen in blue. However, these gases do not always show up in these colors—the colors depend on the temperatures of the gases, too.

Some parts of the nebula are moving away from the central white dwarf at speeds in excess of 300 mi. (500km) per second.

Star death

A star turns into a supernova

It is hard to describe the power of a supernova. A single one can shine brighter than an entire galaxy and can radiate more energy in a few days than the Sun will give out in its entire ten-billion-year lifespan. The explosion of a supermassive star is so powerful that it can accelerate matter to one-tenth of the **speed of light**.

Luckily for us, supernova events are rare. Although there are more than 100 billon stars in our galaxy, only about two of them will turn into supernovae each century. In fact, four centuries have passed since there was one close enough to Earth to be seen with the naked eye.

After being devastated by the flash of light and heat from a supernova, any planets within millions of miles will be blasted by out-flung material.

Supernovae are destructive events, but they are also highly important in the story of the universe. Without them, there might not be any planets. They trigger the collapse of nebulae to form stars. Nuclear fusion inside stars creates the "heavy elements" (elements that are more complex than hydrogen and helium) that supernovae then help spread through the universe. These vital elements form part of all of the worlds we know, and they also form the basic building blocks in the chemistry of living things.

Galactic heart

The center of the Milky Way

The heart of our galaxy is a mysterious place. For a very long time, it was hidden from our view by the stardust that lies between it and our planet. However, although the visible light is cut off, other types of radiation—such as infrared—can pierce through the walls of dust. (On Earth, we can feel some infrared as heat energy.)

The first infrared telescopes were sent into Earth's orbit in the early 1980s so that astronomers could start to build up pictures of the galactic center. In fact, the illustrations on pages 34–35 are based on infrared images of this vast region.

There is a supermassive black hole at the heart of the Milky Way. Black holes themselves do not give out any light, but the matter that falls into them sheds enormous amounts of energy as it slows down from its headlong fall to a dead stop. This freed energy can be seen as a bright burst of light (see above).

Infrared astronomy is a challenge. A great deal of infrared radiation can escape the walls of dust and cross the Galaxy to our solar system. However, almost all of it is then lost at the very end of its journey because it is absorbed by the gases of Earth's atmosphere. But today, now that infrared observatories can be hurled into orbit by rockets, we can truly see the center of the Milky Way.

Local galaxies

Neighboring star systems

If we were able to look out from the edge of our galaxy into the darkness that surrounds it, we would see only a few faint—but fairly large—patches of light. The light is made by the massed stars of other great galaxies. This huge amount of light would be dimmed by the vast distances it has crossed.

Andromeda (at the top of this picture) is the closest large galaxy to our own. It is a little larger, but slightly less massive, than the Milky Way.

The Milky Way and its neighboring galaxies form a cluster called the Local Group. There are countless more such clusters of galaxies sprinkled through the universe, grouped together into even larger associations called **superclusters**. In turn, superclusters form **filaments**. If you were to stand back far enough from such a vast structure to take in the whole of it, its light would be too faint to see.

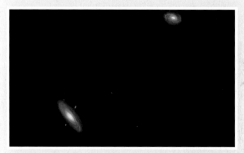

*Like the Milky Way and Andromeda, Triangulum (at the top right of this picture) is a large **spiral galaxy** with smaller galaxies in orbit around it.*

The Virgo Supercluster

Virgo III Groups

NGC 5033

NGC 7582

NGC 6744

NGC 5128

LOCAL GROUP

Sculptor

NGC 1023

M101

M81 Group

Canes Groups

Leo Cluster

Virgo Cluster

NGC 4697

Ursa Major Groups

Dorado

NGC 2997

Fornax Cluster

Eridanus Cluster

The Local Group of Galaxies

Leo I

Leo II

Draco

Ursa Minor

Sextans

IC 10

Andromeda VII

MILKY WAY

Sagittarius

NGC 6822

NGC 147

Large Magellanic Cloud

Small Magellanic Cloud

Andromeda V

NGC 185

Sculptor

Carina

M110

Andromeda (M31)

Fornax

M32

Andromeda II

Andromeda I

Andromeda III

Triangulum

Andromeda IV

LGS 3

Pegasus

Phoenix

IC 1613

Superclusters

Cylinder One: *c.* 100,000,000 LYID

Clusters of galaxies form loose associations called superclusters, and the superclusters themselves form vast shapes called filaments. Between them are gigantic voids that contain almost nothing at all. It is thought that, at an even more enormous scale, there are no more structures. In these endless outer reaches, the universe may become perfectly smooth and regular.

KEY TO MEASUREMENTS:
LYID = light-years in diameter
LHID = light-hours in diameter
c. = *circa* (meaning "approximately")
Diameter = width of each cylinder

Cluster of galaxies

Cylinder Two: *c.* 5,000,000 LYID

Galaxies are grouped together in clusters, such as our Local Group, and all members of a cluster are held close to the others by gravity. Every cluster of galaxies is moving away from all of the others as the universe expands. This expansion began when the universe did, and it seems to be speeding up because of the effects of a mysterious force that scientists refer to as "dark energy."

Our solar system is in the Orion Arm, a spiral arm that is approximately 75,000 light years from the galaxy's edge.

Galaxy

Cylinder Three: *c.* 110,000 LYID

Like perhaps half of the galaxies in the universe, the Milky Way is a spiral shape, with dark and dusty areas between its brighter starry arms. It is more than 100,000 light years in diameter but only about 2,000 light years thick. All galaxies rotate (spin) and are rich in an unknown type of matter known as "dark matter." At the heart of most (or perhaps all) galaxies is a supermassive black hole.

Maps of the universe

Only a few centuries ago, people thought that the universe was a sphere that extended for just a few million miles across its middle, with Earth at its center. Now we know that the universe is more than 65 billion trillion mi. (100 billion trillion km) across. We do not know what its shape is, but we do know that it has no edge: if you were to fly straight out from Earth, at high speed, you would eventually end up back home. We also know that the universe has different structures, at different levels of scale, from places like our solar system to superclusters that are many trillions of times larger

MEASURING DISTANCES USING LIGHT:

Miles are too tiny a unit to be of much use in measuring the universe. *Even our closest neighbor, the Moon, is more than 200,000 mi. (300,000km) away. Instead, we use the time it takes light to cross the distances involved. Light travels at almost 186,000 mi. (300,000km) per second, so the Moon is just over one "light-second" away.*

Planetary system

Cylinder Four: *c.* 12 LHID

Many stars have planets and smaller objects in orbit around them, which together form planetary systems. We call ours the solar system. We do not know how typical it is, but it seems likely that many others also contain gas giants, rocky planets, comets, small worlds, and dust and gas left over from the formation of these systems.

The Milky Way Galaxy

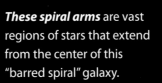

Sagittarius

These spiral arms are vast regions of stars that extend from the center of this "barred spiral" galaxy.

The Solar System

SOLAR INTERSTELLAR NEIGHBORHOOD

Halley's comet (orbiting the Sun)

Pluto (a dwarf planet)

Saturn

Jupiter   *Earth*   *Sun*   *Mercury*

Kuiper belt   *Venus*   *Mars*   *Neptune*

Uranus

The distance across the solar system is roughly 8.4 light hours.

Please note: *the planets and their relative orbits are not to scale.*

Glossary

Words in **bold italics** refer to other glossary entries that you will find on these two pages.

ammonia
A strong-smelling gas made up of *nitrogen* and *hydrogen*.

asteroid
A small, rocky, airless world.

atmosphere
A layer of gases around a planet.

atom
A basic unit of matter: the smallest particle of a chemical *element*.

aurora
A glow of light over the poles of a *planet*, caused by charged particles from a *star* being trapped by the planet's magnetism and colliding with molecules in its upper *atmosphere*.

black hole
An object with such high *density* and *gravity* that even light cannot escape.

brown dwarf
A *star* whose *mass* is so low that no *nuclear reactions* can occur at its core.

cell
One or more of these makes up every living thing on Earth.

chemical
A substance in which groups of *atoms* are joined in a repeating pattern.

comet
A large lump of grit and ice that travels on a long *orbit* around the Sun. Comets sometimes deposit water on planets when they collide with them.

core
The central part of an object such as a moon, planet, or star.

crust
The outermost layer of a rocky world.

density
The amount of matter (stuff) that is contained within a particular volume. (Volume is the space an object takes up.) The density of water, for example, is about 62 lb./cu. ft. (1,000kg/m³).

dwarf planet
A small world that *orbits* the Sun or another *star*, with enough *gravity* to be spherical (ball-shaped) or nearly so.

element
A pure substance that cannot be made any simpler than it is already.

filament
1) A long, thin stream of gas on the surface of the Sun. 2) The name for the largest type of structure in the universe, made of billions of *galaxies*.

galaxy
A large group of *stars* and other material, held together by *gravity*.

geyser
A powerful, natural burst of water and steam from the surface of a world.

gravity
The invisible force of attraction between objects in the universe, created by the *mass* of those objects. For example, the Moon *orbits* Earth because Earth is more massive.

helium
The second lightest and second most common *element*, used on Earth to make balloons rise into the air.

hydrocarbons
Substances made by combining carbon and *hydrogen*.

hydrogen
The lightest and the most commonly occurring *element* in the universe.

ice cap
The frozen region surrounding the north and south poles of worlds such as Earth and Mars.

infrared
Invisible *radiation* that is created by warm objects.

Kuiper belt
A vast region of *comet*like objects that lies beyond the *orbit* of Neptune.

magnetic field
The region around a magnet, such as around the core of a *star* or *planet*, where the force of magnetism can affect other magnets.

mass
The amount of matter that something contains. The mass of objects creates the effects of *gravity*.

methane
A gas made of *hydrogen* and carbon.

molten rock
Rock so hot that it has become a liquid.

moon
A world that *orbits* a *planet*.

nebula
A cloudlike mass of gas and/or dust.

neutron star
An object that sometimes remains after a massive *star* has died. Extremely dense, with a powerful *magnetic field*.

neutronium
A material made of highly crushed *atoms*, from which *neutron stars* are composed.

nitrogen
The most common gas in Earth's *atmosphere*.

nuclear fuel
The material used to produce energy in a *star's* core or a nuclear reactor.

nuclear fusion
A process in which light *atoms* join together to make heavier ones, releasing energy as they do so.

nuclear reaction
What happens when the nuclei (cores) of atoms are forced so close together that they either break up or combine.

Oort cloud
The outermost area of the *solar system*, made up of distant, icy, *comet*like objects.

orbit
The path of one object around another in space, maintained by *gravity*.

organism
A living animal, plant, or single-celled life form.

oxygen
The gas in our *atmosphere* that we breathe in to enable our body's *cells* and tissues to function.

planet
A large world in *orbit* around the Sun or another *star*.

planetary nebula
An expanding cloud of glowing gas around the remains of a dead *star*.

pulsar
A spinning *neutron star*.

radiation
Energy that travels through space, such as light, radio waves, and *infrared*.

solar system
The Sun, its orbiting *planets*, and other objects that travel around it.

space probe
A spacecraft with no crew, launched into space to explore other worlds.

speed of light
Almost 186,300 mi. (300,000km) per second.

spiral galaxy
A large galaxy with brightly-glowing arms extending from a central core.

star
A large object in space, usually glowing because of the release of energy inside it.

supercluster
A loose group of clusters of *galaxies*.

supermassive star
A star with about 50 times more mass than our Sun.

supernova
A huge explosion in space, produced by the collapse of a single, massive *star* or a sudden change in a pair of stars.

trillion
A million million (1,000,000,000,000).

white dwarf
The shrunken remains of the *core* of a dead *star*.

yellow dwarf
Another name for a *star* like our Sun.

Useful websites

Look online to see new astronomical discoveries and how scientists map the structure of the universe.

An Atlas of the Universe
www.atlasoftheuniverse.com/

Astronomy Picture of the Day
http://apod.nasa.gov/apod/

***Celestia* space simulator**
www.shatters.net/celestia/

From atoms to the whole universe
http://powersof10.com/

NASA's Kepler mission homepage
http://kepler.nasa.gov/

Zoom in on the Milky Way galaxy
www.gigagalaxyzoom.org/B.html

Places to visit

Visit these inspiring places to discover more about the history of astronomy, our exploration of the universe, and the dazzling new technology that will expand our knowledge in the future.

Kennedy Space Center
SR 405
Kennedy Space Center, FL 32899
http://kennedyspacecenter.com

Smithsonian National Air and Space Museum
Independence Ave. at 6th Street, SW
Washington, DC 20560
(202) 633-1000
http://www.nasm.si.edu

Griffith Observatory
2800 East Observatory Road
Los Angeles, CA 90027
(213) 473-0800
http://www.griffithobservatory.org

Index